# EXPLORER BOOKS

# POISONOUS CREATURES

by
Julia L. Andrews

to my favorite mammals,
Joan and Peter

Published by The Trumpet Club
666 Fifth Avenue, New York, New York 10103

ISBN: 0-440-84290-5

Produced by Parachute Press, Inc.
Printed in the United States of America
September 1990

10 9 8 7 6 5 4 3
CW

PHOTOGRAPH CREDITS

*p. 25: top,* Anthony Bannister/Animals Animals; *bottom,* © 1979 Mandal Ranjit/Photo
Researchers, Inc.   *p. 26:* © Tom McHugh, 1973/Photo Researchers, Inc.   *p. 27:* Leonard
Lee Rue III/Animals Animals.   *p. 28: top,* © Raymond A. Mendez/Animals Animals; *bottom,* Steinhart Aquarium, © 1974 Tom McHugh/Photo Researchers, Inc.   *p. 29:* Verna R.
Johnston/Photo Researchers, Inc.   *p. 30: top,* © Carl Roessler/Animals Animals; *bottom,*
© A. W. Ambler from National Audubon Society/Photo Researchers, Inc.   *p. 31:* Verna R.
Johnston/Photo Researchers, Inc.   *p. 32: top,* Michael Fogden/Animals Animals; *bottom,*
© Terry G. Murphy/Animals Animals.

*Cover:* © Zig Leszczynski/Animals Animals.

# **Contents**

# Introduction

## Deadly Brew

Welcome to the world of poisonous animals. You might think of poison as a bottle with a skull and crossbones on the label, off limits on the highest shelf. But if some animals didn't have this special weapon, they'd starve to death. Or they'd be killed and eaten up themselves!

Poison isn't just liquid from a bee stinger or a snake fang. Saliva in your mouth is poison, too. Poison is any chemical that destroys living things.

Each kind of poison is deadly to certain life forms. Your saliva will kill bacteria, but it won't hurt *you* at all. Every poisonous animal has its own poison that suits its needs. The rattlesnake eats mice, so it needs a poison that kills mice.

How do poisons work? Some paralyze muscles, or make the victim's heart stop, or make it bleed to death. Others make blood clot in the victim's veins. If too little blood reaches the brain or other body parts, the victim dies.

Fangs, stingers, claws, teeth, tentacles, and spines are all special devices that animals use to inject poison into the victim. When poison is injected, it is called venom. Snakes, spiders, and other animals that inject venom are called venomous animals.

Poisonous animals have lived on this planet for millions of years. They were around before humans, woolly mammoths, dinosaurs, or the Ice Age. Snakes, snails, spiders, lizards, frogs, insects, fish, and even a few mammals evolved into poisonous creatures over millions of years. The only group of animals on earth that doesn't have a poisonous member is birds.

Some people think the world would be better without poisonous animals. But if there were no poisonous creatures, our world would be a very different place. Without venomous snakes, rats and mice would be *everywhere!* If there were no bees, there'd be no honey or sweet-smelling flowers. If there were no spiders, we'd be living in a cloud of flies. Poisonous animals get rid of creatures that eat our crops. They help keep nature in balance.

# 1

## Cold-blooded Killers

A snake has no arms or legs. It can't grab or chase after its fast-moving four-legged meals, yet it eats animals that bite. If the snake is going to triumph over its prey, it must win the fight quickly. Otherwise, the meal will run away. Or worse, the mouse will sink its teeth into the snake's spine. So how does the snake catch—and kill—a mouse in a minute or two?

The snake uses two very powerful weapons: fangs and venom. Of the 3,000 types of snakes in the world, only 300 are venomous. One of the most well known venomous snakes is the *rattlesnake,* the deadliest snake in North America.

Rattlesnakes are reptiles, which means they're cold-blooded. They eat small, warm-blooded animals, such as mice, rats, and rabbits. Like a heat-seeking missile, the rattlesnake easily finds warm things in the dark. Pits like small holes under its eyes "see" heat as bright, glowing spots. So it's easy for a snake to find a tasty, warm mouse on a cold desert night. The mouse glows in the dark! To a snake, you look like an enormous glowing UFO. Snakes that have these pits are called *pit vipers*.

A rattlesnake also finds prey with a flick of its tongue. With each flick, the snake tastes and smells the air for the scent of its prey. The tongue also works like an ear. It feels vibrations that make sounds.

When a rattlesnake senses that its next meal is near, it whips out a pair of sharp fangs filled with killer venom. They have jagged edges to help dig into flesh. Most of the time, the fangs are folded up in pockets inside the snake's mouth. (The snake can't close its mouth when the long fangs are extended.) After a few uses, the fangs drop out. A new pair quickly pops into place. People who have been bitten by a rattlesnake say the fangs feel like hot needles being jabbed into their skin.

The rattlesnake strikes the fastest of all venomous snakes. You can't see it bite. It moves too fast for human eyes to see! It lunges at prey, injects the venom, and pulls back to its original position *in less than a single second*. That's about as long as it takes you to blink.

The rattlesnake, like other venomous snakes, usually strikes prey in the chest, close to the animal's heart. Somehow, venomous snakes know

4

exactly how much venom it takes to kill each animal. A little mouse gets a tiny dose. A fat rabbit gets a bigger dose. It takes too much time and energy to make a new batch of venom, so snakes try to conserve it. That's why they never inject all their venom at one time. They never know when they'll need to strike next!

Like all venomous snakes, a rattlesnake uses its fangs and venom for one main purpose: supper. It takes a lot of energy to catch a meal, so snakes are picky about who they bite. Each meal has to last a long time. Rattlers usually feed about every two months. But if the meal is a big squirrel, the snake won't eat for a year!

A rattlesnake isn't interested in eating human beings. People are much too big to swallow! A snake will only strike a human if it's scared. When it strikes in defense, it doesn't control how much venom it injects. An unlucky person might get a big dose, or none at all.

Venom works on animals in different ways. Some venoms make the victim bleed a lot. Others make blood clot. Some venoms cause muscle cramps or make muscles relax too much. No two snakes have the same kind of venom. Snakes need different venoms because they hunt different animals. For example, venom that stops a rat may not work on a fish.

One teaspoon of rattlesnake venom can kill a human being. Like all snake venom, rattlesnake venom is a mixture of proteins and other substances. It digests food, just as human saliva does. But before venom starts digesting, it kills.

To do its job, venom has to be in the blood. That's why snakes have fangs. If you drank snake venom, it wouldn't hurt you. The worst thing you'd feel would be tingling on your lips. But if it got in your blood, you'd feel *terrible.*

When venom first enters a victim's system, the area around the bite feels numb. The numbness usually means that the snake injected a lot of venom. Then the victim feels faint and sweaty. It gets blurry vision. Now the venom really goes to work. It stops the brain from receiving and sending messages to the nerves and muscles. The victim becomes paralyzed and it can't run away.

Venom can also make a victim's blood flow very, very quickly. This makes sure that the venom reaches every part of the animal's insides. Gushing blood brings on death when poisoned blood fills the victim's lungs instead of air. It can't breathe. It drowns in its own blood. Meanwhile, the venom starts digesting the dead creature's insides. This makes the meal easier for the snake to devour.

Not all small animals are easy prey for snakes. If a rattlesnake tries to kill a possum for supper, the snake will go hungry. Possums not only are immune to venom, they'll even eat rattlers and other venomous snakes!

Rattlesnakes don't usually bite people. They are shy creatures that hide under rocks and bushes.

Sometimes they'll swim or climb trees for a quick getaway. If they can't hide from you, they'll shake their rattle to scare you away. (The rattle is made of the same stuff as your fingernails.)

If the loud hiss of its rattle doesn't make you run, the snake will bite. Will you drop dead if a rattlesnake bites you? Probably not. Rattlesnake venom is basically mild. In the United States, only twelve people a year die from the bite of venomous snakes. Twice as many people die each year from bee and wasp stings. And thousands of people die in car accidents. So your chances of being killed by a rattlesnake are very, very slim. Even so, if you meet one on a path, leave it alone and walk away *slowly*.

## Red and Black, Friend of Jack

Almost every snake you see slithering through the grass in North America is nonpoisonous. Once in a while, one of these snakes may try to bite you. But they can't kill you — they don't have any venom. The only venomous snakes in North America are the rattlers, the water moccasins, and the coral snakes.

The *coral snake* has a very deadly bite. Its short fangs are always extended. It wraps its mouth around a victim so its fangs will get a firm grip. It doesn't inject venom in a quick shot like the rattlesnake does. It chews its venom in to make sure the venom really gets under the prey's skin.

7

The coral snake has beautiful red, yellow, and black stripes. Birds and other predators won't attack because those stripes mean danger! Several nonvenomous snakes with colored stripes take advantage of this fact. Predators are fooled into thinking these mild snakes are killers.

The way to tell the killers from the pretenders is by examining the order of the stripes. In many species, if the red and black stripes are next to each other, it's a pretender. If the red and yellow stripes are next to each other, it's the killer. Red and black, friend of Jack. Red and yellow, kill the fellow.

## Boomslangs in Space

The tree-climbing snakes of Africa are extremely deadly. Because they live in trees, they rarely bite humans. When they do bite a person, it's usually because the person has been trying to catch the snake while up in a tree.

Whenever it gets hungry, it quickly slinks up a tall tree trunk in search of birds' nests. If *you* tried a fast climb to a high spot, you might faint. Your blood would rush from your brain to your feet. When your brain doesn't get enough blood, it shuts down.

This is true for snakes, too, but the *African boomslang,* one of the deadliest of the tree-climbing snakes, doesn't faint because of a built-in super-tight gravity suit. Astronauts wear these suits in space to keep blood from flowing downward to their feet.

One dose of the venom of a boomslang can easily kill a few people. Unlike other venomous snakes, the boomslang can't inject venom. It has fangs in the back of its mouth that work more like regular teeth than needles. Venom flows down the fangs in grooves on the side of each fang when the boomslang chews its victim.

When it gets to the treetop and finds a tasty bird, the boomslang wraps its huge jaws around its prey to grind in its venom. Death from this snakebite doesn't happen quickly. A bird will slowly bleed to death as the venom digests the bird's insides. Blood oozes from its mouth, eyes, ears, and any other body opening.

## The Snake That Killed the Queen

Deadly snakes live all over the African continent. But the one that kills more people than any other snake in Africa is the *puff adder.* This giant snake grows up to 5 feet long and has strong venom, but it's not the strongest venom among the deadly snakes. So what makes the adder the number one killer?

Two things—its habitat and its personality. Puff adders live everywhere in Africa except the rain forests and the desert. They tend to live in big fields and farmlands—places where people live. Many teenage boys in farming villages get puff adder bites because they take care of animals in the fields.

The puff adder crawls into villages at night in search of rats and mice that nest in crops. If an unsuspecting person stumbles over the snake in the dark, the adder won't budge. It will bite.

Cleopatra, the beautiful queen of ancient Egypt, knew how deadly the adder is. She killed herself by holding an adder to her chest. One quick bite, and the queen was dead.

### Fantastic Fangs

The *gaboon viper* has the longest fangs of all venomous snakes. Its fangs are 2 inches long! Those fangs would be deadly even if they didn't have venom in them! Like the cobras, mambas, and adders, the gaboon is a giant snake. It can grow up to 7 feet long, and has a head 5 inches wide.

When people think of snake venom, they imagine instant death. For mice and other small mammals, venom *does* bring on instant death. But this doesn't happen in humans. A person can die from snake venom, of course, but usually it will take a few minutes. If a gaboon viper bites a person, he or she *can* die instantly. With its gigantic fangs, the gaboon gets deep down into a victim's muscles and organs. The venom doesn't have to go far to do its damage. Unlike the fierce puff adder, the gaboon viper is very mild-mannered. It only bites when its life is threatened.

The gaboon viper has a big mouth. It can eat small antelope. With a mouth that big, this snake could easily gobble up small monkeys and human babies. But it doesn't. No venomous snake in the world today eats two-legged creatures like humans, monkeys, or apes.

## Deep-sea Terror

The Roman emperor Nero had a terrible temper. He would throw prisoners into pools filled with hungry *sea snakes*. The prisoners died from the snakes' deadly venom.

*Herpetologists* (people who study snakes) think Nero must have starved the snakes to make them so aggressive. Sea snakes usually ignore humans. They're smart hunters who only attack bite-size animals. A diver in Panama knows that for a fact. He swam into a raft of thousands of sea snakes floating together. Not a single snake tried to bite him.

Sea snakes live around reefs in the Indian and Pacific oceans. Sea snakes have super-strong venom—one species has venom that's 50 times stronger than the king cobra's. Sea snakes need fast-acting venom to stop fast fish from swimming away.

If you had a contest with a sea snake to see who could hold their breath underwater the longest, the sea snake would easily win. The sea snake needs to breathe air through its lungs just like other snakes. However, this snake has extra-big lungs. It can stay underwater for almost eight hours!

Imagine shooting a bow and arrow underwater. How could you aim at the bull's-eye with waves pushing you around? The sea snake has this same problem when it tries to strike prey. But its thick, flat tail acts like a built-in anchor. With the help of this tail, the snake can stay still long enough to aim its fangs and hit the bull's-eye: fresh fish.

## Down Under and Deadly

Want to steer clear of venomous snakes? Then don't go to Australia. Many of the world's deadliest snakes live on this continent. (No one knows why, but Australia has all kinds of deadly animals.) The top killer snakes on the continent are the *taipan* and the *eastern brown snake*. It takes only a drop or two of their venoms to kill someone.

The taipan is the jackhammer of venomous snakes. Say the word "jackhammer." That's how long it takes a taipan to give three or four lethal bites. The taipan bites so fast, people don't realize what's happening until it's too late. With every bite, the snake injects a dose of nerve poison. People almost always die from taipan bites.

The eastern brown snake would do great in gym class. It jumps off the ground when it strikes.

Many times it bites people above the knee. The eastern brown snake is a little more than 3 feet long, which isn't very long for a snake. But don't let size fool you. Drop for drop, brown snake venom is many times stronger than cobra venom.

Brown snakes and taipans don't sit around waiting to bite humans. They spend their time hunting rats and mice in rural areas. Farmers find them hiding under barns or crawling around wheat bins. The snakes actually help farmers. Rats and mice are farm pests that eat crops. By gobbling up these pests, snakes save people from going hungry!

## Big, Bad, and Fast

You're going to run in a track meet, but you're not going to compete with kids from another school. You're going to race against a *black mamba snake* for 1 mile. You have two feet; the snake has no feet. Who will win?

If you're in very good shape, you should be able to run 7 miles an hour. How fast can the snake move? 7 miles an hour—*just as fast as you!* The black mamba is the fastest snake in the world.

Africa is a place with many deadly snakes. The deadliest—and the longest—of them all is the black mamba. It looks like a very skinny piece of rope and grows over 14 feet long. The mamba is quite a killer. Two drops of its venom are enough to kill ten people. Its venom turns your body into bloody mush and attacks your nerves, muscles, brain, liver, and lungs. In just a short time, it can do a lot of damage. If a black mamba ever shows up at your track meet, drop out of the race!

## King of the Snakes

The deadliest snake *in the world* is the *king cobra.* It can kill an enormous elephant. No other snake can do that! King cobra venom isn't as strong as the venoms of sea snakes or the Australian snakes. However, those other snakes only inject a tiny bit of killer juice when they bite. The king cobra injects tremendous amounts of venom when it strikes.

The king cobra is huge and powerful. It grows up to 19 feet long. Its head alone is as big as a man's fist. In a battle with another snake, the king cobra always wins. One fast stab of venom, and the fight is finished.

King cobras live in the jungles of Asia, far away from villages and people. In comparison to some other snakes, king cobras are mild-mannered. If a person surprises the snake, it would rather flee than fight. Once a man stepped on a king cobra in a field, and the snake hissed. As soon as the man lifted his foot, the snake slid away to hide as fast as possible. Because this snake is so gigantic, you have to give it plenty of room to flee. Like any other snake, the king cobra bites when it can't escape.

The *African cobra,* which is related to the

king, has an interesting way of keeping trespass-
ers out. The cobra has fantastic aim and spits
venom at anyone who invades its turf. It can
shoot into the eyes of someone 9 feet away. This
spit is very painful and blinds people. Cobras are
killers—there's no doubt about it.

## First Aid for Snakebites

Follow these tips if you want to avoid getting
a snakebite. When you're in snake country, look
before you step. Don't poke your hands between
rocks unless you can see very clearly that a
snake isn't there. Wear thick, high-topped shoes
and long pants. Most fangs can't cut through
tough material. If you're camping out for the
night, sleep in a tent or off the ground. If you're
*on* the ground, a snake can crawl inside your
sleeping bag!

If a snake bites you, walk—don't run—to the
nearest doctor. When you run, your blood (and
the venom) circulates faster throughout your
body. In the old days, people advised wrapping a
band very tightly above the bite. If the wrap is
too tight, it will cut off all circulation, which is
very dangerous. The bandage should be loose
enough to fit your finger underneath. If you have
a snakebite kit, use the suction cup to suck out
venom. (These cups only work for bites that
aren't very deep.) Do not cut the bite open! You'll
infect the bite with even more germs. And try
not to panic.

# 2

## The Truth About Miss Muffet's Monster

Remember Miss Muffet who sat on a tuffet? When that spider sat down beside her, she ran away. But that little spider couldn't have hurt her! (By the way, Miss Muffet was a real girl. Her father, Thomas Muffet, studied spiders in England.) Sure, the spider was venomous, but its venom is used to trap small insects, not big kids.

Are spiders insects? No. Insects have six legs, four wings, and two antennae. Spiders have eight legs, no wings, and no antennae. They weave silky webs and have fangs. Insects can't weave webs and don't have fangs. However, both insects and spiders have jointed legs and hard outer shells called *exoskeletons.*

Spiders belong to a group of animals called *arachnids.* You can tell an arachnid from an insect by counting the number of body segments.

Spiders, scorpions, ticks, and mites have two body segments. Ants and other insects have three body segments.

There are at least 37,000 species of spiders in the world. You can find them in many kinds of habitats, from scorching hot to freezing cold places. Some even live on top of Mt. Everest! If you counted every spider in 1 acre of meadow, you'd find about *2 million!*

All spiders are venomous, except for one family. With so many of these deadly monsters around, you'd think people would die from their bites all the time. But only a few spiders can really harm humans. Most spider venom isn't toxic enough to make a person very sick. Besides, most spiders don't have fangs that are long enough— or sharp enough—to jab through human skin.

While most spider venom won't hurt humans, it's a deadly hunting tool. A few drops of powerful venom lets spiders catch big meals. Spiders are meat-eaters, or *carnivores.* (You're an *omnivore,* which means you eat meat and plants.) Usually, spiders eat animals much larger than themselves. In Brazil, some tarantulas feed on birds, lizards, even small poisonous snakes! However, most spiders feed on large insects.

## Small but Mighty Hunters

If spiders don't capture their victims in a flash,

they can become victims themselves. When a creature comes close, the spider quickly stabs its fangs into the animal's nerves. The venom doesn't kill on the spot. It instantly paralyzes the animal and starts to digest the animal's insides. The animal dies as its innards turn to mush. The spider then sucks up supper through its straw-like mouth. (Spiders can't chew, so they don't actually "bite." They stab and suck.)

Venom alone isn't enough to help a spider survive. Its other survival tool is silk, the stuff webs are made of. Spiders can do some amazing things with their flimsy nets. Circular webs like the ones you see in bushes or dusty rooms can be 18 feet wide! That's only one of many different kinds of webs. The *purse web spider* spins a web shaped like a tube sock. It spends its entire life sealed up inside the web! Another family, the *nursery web spiders,* protect their babies in webs shaped like tents.

Though they might seem delicate with their beautiful patterns and shapes, spiderwebs are made from the strongest fibers in nature. A strand of silk is as strong as a strand of steel. Spiders have several glands to make different types of silk for different purposes. Some silks are smooth, some are sticky. The silk is used to hunt and to protect eggs. Webs are made of both sticky and smooth silk. Insects get caught in the sticky silk of the web, and the spider has a meal.

Other animal hunters have excellent sight and

hearing to help them locate food. But spiders have rotten eyesight. They don't even have ears! So how do they locate their prey? They have a fantastic sense of touch. Little hairs on their legs work like wind vanes to figure out the direction of the tiniest vibration or air movement. Once spiders have this information, they find prey quickly in their webs.

Why don't spiders get caught in their own webs? Because they hang away from the sticky stuff with strong claws. They also have oil on their legs that won't stick to silk.

Webs are just one way spiders use silk to catch prey. The *spitting spider* spits silk strands in zigzag patterns over a bug. The strands trap the bug in a sticky net. Now it's easy for the spider to stab the bug full of killer juice.

The *bola spider* has a unique way of finding a tasty meal of moths. Every day it hangs from a tree and spins out a silk line with a big blob of gum on the end. The bola sends out a special "moth" perfume to attract insects. Then it swings its "fishing" line at any moth that happens to come near. If the spider has good aim, the gum blob sticks to the moth.

The *European water spider* lives in ponds and lakes. It spends most of its life underwater, and builds a diving air tank with its silk. It even raises its babies underwater. But spiders don't have gills like fish. They have to breathe air to survive. While underwater, the spider weaves a silk patch. Then it blows air bubbles from its abdomen and wraps the patch around the bubbles. Once it's finished, the tank is shaped like a bell. When the spider isn't hunting, it stays underwater in the air tank. However, when it catches insects in the pond, it feeds *out* of the water. Water dilutes the spider's venom and it becomes useless.

A *fishing spider* can walk on water without sinking. It floats on leaves in a pond in search of food. Like any good fisherman, it patiently dips its rod—its leg—into the pond and waits for a bite. When a small fish nibbles on its leg (thinking the leg is a tasty insect), the spider makes its deadly move. A fishing spider doesn't weave a web. It belongs to a large group of spiders that hunt without the help of silk. Another member of this group is the *jumping spider*. It hunts for food just like a cat does. It stalks the victim, pounces on the animal, and delivers its deadly bite. These spiders can jump 40 times their own body length. If you could do that, you'd be able to leap over two football fields!

The venoms of most spiders bring quick death to their victims, but can't harm you. Of the millions of spiders in the world, very few can deliver fatal bites to humans.

But if a *black widow* sat down beside Miss Muffet, she'd have good reason to worry! Black widows *are* deadly. You can tell a widow from other black spiders by the red hourglass shape on its undersides. This famous "monster" is found in warm climates. Only two dangerous spiders live in the United States: the black widow and the *brown recluse*.

The female black widow is one of the most poisonous animals around. A small drop of her venom can make a 200-pound man sick in no time flat. Her venom is 15 times stronger than rattlesnake venom. The male black widow doesn't have very much venom and hardly ever bites.

Black widows are very shy. They bite humans only in self-defense and live in dark places.

Like the black widow, the brown recluse is shy. Its venom isn't as strong as the black widow's, but watch out! Its bite is very, very painful, takes over a month to heal, and leaves a huge scar.

Black widows and brown recluses are scary spiders, but the *scariest* spider is the *Australian funnel-web spider.* As you can tell from its name, this spider spins a funnel-shaped web that it attaches to rocks and tree roots. It hides from its prey in the tube at the end of the funnel. When an insect is near, the spider crawls out of its tube and tangles the victim in its sticky, silky web.

The funnel-web spider has venom that is stronger than a black widow's. When the female is very upset, she dangles a large glob of venom from the tip of her fangs to scare curious creatures away. The funnel-web has huge fangs that can bite through a child's fingernail—no other spider can do that.

One spider with a nasty reputation is the *tarantula*. Everyone thinks it's creepy. It looks mean. It's big and hairy. With its legs spread out, it's almost as big as a Frisbee!

But tarantulas aren't dangerous, even though they're related to the funnel-web. Their venom won't hurt you. In fact, they make great pets. Lots of kids around the country now have tarantulas as classroom pets. Once in a while, if a tarantula is very irritated, it might toss a furball at an annoying animal or human hand. The ball is made of hooked hairs covered with a poison, and it can give you a rash. However, tarantulas don't toss furballs at humans very often.

Many people are still terrified of tarantulas no matter what you tell them. Knowing how scared people are of these hairy beasts, a jewelry store owner in San Francisco used tarantulas to guard his store. The spiders spent their nights in the jewelry cases, climbing around diamonds and gold. No thief was brave enough to steal the goods!

In the wild, the tarantula is a tough fighter. It easily captures animals much larger than itself such as lizards and snakes. One animal it won't eat is the tiny *narrow-mouthed toad*. In fact, the tarantula protects this toad from hungry snakes! The toads live in the tarantula's burrow, along with the spider's offspring. If a snake dares to poke into the burrow in search of food, the tarantula scuttles up to the snake and shows off its fangs in a frightening way. The toad hops under the spider's fangs and waits for the snake to slither away. While the tarantula protects the toads, the toads protect the tarantula's young. The toads eat ants that invade the burrow in search of a meal of spider babies.

A tarantula can scare off snakes, but it isn't so lucky with wasps. The *tarantula hawk wasp* stings and paralyzes the tarantula. When the spider is completely drugged, the wasp drags it to its own burrow. The wasp buries the spider alive as food for its soon-to-be-hatched larvae. When the larvae hatch, they're very hungry. The live spider is their first meal.

Other enemies of the spider include birds, insects, and even other spiders! Spiders protect themselves against predators in several ways. The females produce many eggs to make sure that some young will survive. Many spiders use camouflage as a defense. They have coloring that allows them to blend into the backgrounds so they can hide from hunters. If a predator grabs a spider by the leg, the spider breaks off its leg to get free. A special mechanism stops the spider from bleeding to death. If you could see the spider's blood, it would look pale blue. The spider's leg grows back eventually.

# Night Stalkers

The scorpion, a relative of the spider, is one of the spider's worst enemies. Spiders are a favorite meal for scorpions. They are arachnids, just like spiders. They live in warm, dry desert regions all around the world. In the United States, you find them out west in Arizona, California, and other dry areas.

A scorpion looks like a crab. It has eight legs, a pair of pincers, and a pair of large claws that it uses to catch and crush prey. Though it has six to twelve eyes, it can't see very well. It breathes through holes in its abdomen. At the end of its tail is a very poisonous stinger that has made scorpions famous.

The sting of a *North African scorpion* can kill an adult in 4 hours. It can kill a dog in just 7 minutes. When you think how strong a scorpion's venom is, no wonder people avoid them! Surprisingly, the deadliest scorpions are the smallest ones. Species that have very thin, weak pincers have very strong venom. The larger species that have large, strong pincers have weak venom. A sting from a large scorpion will be very painful, but it won't kill you.

Scorpions won't sting humans unless provoked. They don't even use their stingers when hunting unless the victim puts up a good fight. Then the scorpion lifts its long tail, zaps its prey with the stinger, and waits for the venom to

A black mamba snake protects eggs in its nest. Uncoiled, this snake measures over 14 feet long!

The king cobra feeds mostly on other snakes. Its head alone is as big as a man's fist.

A red diamondback rattlesnake whips out a pair of sharp fangs filled with killer venom.

An African forest cobra slithers through the grass, ready to spit blinding venom. The cobra can shoot as far as 9 feet!

A small drop of female black widow spider venom can make a 200-pound man sick.

The emperor scorpion is the largest of its species. Its sting is very painful, but not deadly.

The tarantula looks like a big hairy monster—but it makes a great pet!

The puffer fish puffs out its body when it is scared.

Little clownfish find a home among the sea anemone's poisonous tentacles.

The black and coral, beady-skinned Gila monster is the only poisonous lizard in the United States.

The tiny, brightly-colored dart-poison frog sweats a deadly substance to protect itself from danger in the rain forest.

Don't go near a hive of killer bees—a swarm of them will chase you for over an hour!

work. Like spider venom, the scorpion's venom instantly turns the victim's insides into stew. The scorpion spends hours sucking up its tasty treat.

During the day, scorpions hide under rocks. When nighttime comes, they come out to hunt and mate. Scorpions are nocturnal creatures. Scientists have found that their bodies glow in the dark when you shine an ultraviolet light on them. Like their spider relatives, scorpions don't have well-developed senses. Even so, they're excellent hunters. They can even find buried insects in the dark. How do they do it? Through special receptors on their eight legs, scorpions can detect the slightest vibrations in the sand.

If a scorpion feels the movement of a cockroach through the grains of desert sand, it quickly turns and crawls in the direction of the movement. It opens and closes its strong claws in hopes of catching its prey. No luck. It waits for the animal to move again. When the cockroach moves, the scorpion quickly moves in the new direction, clicking its pincers as it goes. Success! It finds the cockroach burrowed under the sand.

Scorpions are very resourceful animals. They eat until they almost burst when there are plenty of insects and spiders around. The extra bulk makes their hard outer shells stretch out. Scorpions convert the extra food into carbohydrates, which give the body energy. When there's a food shortage, scorpions shut their metabolism down. (Your metabolism is everything your body does to stay alive.) Scorpions can go for a full year without food, living off stored carbohydrates.

Scorpions have another interesting survival trick when food is in short supply—they eat each other.

Eating each other may sound strange, but it's how scorpions survive. They've been around for hundreds of millions of years. They were the first poisonous animals on earth.

# 3

# Sea Monsters

You don't have to stay on dry land to find poisonous creatures. Deadly monsters live in oceans, too! Just like snakes and spiders in the woods, poisonous sea creatures sting, bite, stab, and zap venom to stay alive.

## Jelly Giants

In the freezing cold seas by the Arctic Circle lives a creature that's longer than a blue whale and wider than a small car. It doesn't have a heart, a brain, bones, or fins. Its body looks like an enormous bowl of clear, blue jelly. More than a thousand stinging tentacles hang from its head; each one is longer than half a football field. It drifts in the ocean and stings anything it bumps into. Sound like the Loch Ness Monster? It's not. It's the *giant Arctic jellyfish*, one of nature's real monsters.

Jellyfish aren't fish, and they aren't made of jelly. They are 94 percent water! They belong to the same group of animals as the *sea anemones*. Jellyfish have as many as 1,200 stringy tentacles lined with *millions* of venom-filled darts. These darts shoot out anytime the tentacles touch food or foe. The venom paralyzes the victim. The darts also help keep the victim tangled in the tentacles.

Jellyfish eat shrimp, crabs, and small fish. Sometimes they eat other jellyfish. A jellyfish eats and gets rid of wastes with its mouth, the only opening in the creature's body.

Jellyfish spend their lives floating on the water's surface. They drift with the currents and wind. Some push themselves along by pumping water out of their bulb.

Some scientists think bigger jellyfish are found in colder waters because the small creatures that jellyfish feed on are much more abundant in cold waters.

Most jellyfish don't have strong enough venom to hurt you seriously. Jellyfish venom is used to hunt prey much smaller than humans. But there's one jellyfish that can kill you in 30 seconds. It has a few names: *sea wasp, box jellyfish*, or *fire medusa*. (Medusa is the name of a Greek goddess who had snakes instead of hair on her head.) Some sea wasps are as small as grapes. Others are as large as grapefruit. Their 8-foot tentacles have 516,000 darts *per square inch.*

Like many other deadly sea creatures, sea wasps live near Australia. Lifeguards who patrol beaches in sea-wasp areas wear pantyhose to protect themselves!

The *Portuguese man-of-war* is not a jellyfish. It's a look-alike relative called a *hydrozoan.* A man-of-war looks like one animal, but it's really a colony of several tiny animals. Every member of the colony has a job to do. Some help capture prey and some help digest food. The man-of-war has a large bag filled with gas that acts like a sail. The bag keeps the colony afloat. The 50-foot tentacles stay underwater. It's the most poisonous sea creature in North America.

## Poisonous Partners

*Clownfish* come in many bright colors — orange, yellow, violet, and hot pink. The little clownfish is a slow swimmer. It doesn't have fangs. It doesn't have stingers. It doesn't seem to have any way to protect itself against big, hungry fish. If clownfish are such easy prey, why aren't they all eaten up?

The clownfish has a very deadly weapon — the *sea anemone.* These purple, pink, red, blue, and green creatures grow on rocks in ocean coral reefs. People think sea anemones are plants, but they aren't. Sea anemones are animals that don't have backbones. They're *invertebrates.* What look like rubber bands are hundreds of venomous tentacles, long, flexible organs used for touching and grasping. These tentacles provide a safe home for clownfish. Clownfish do a little dance before they enter an anemone. They gently wipe their fins and bellies against the tentacles to cover themselves with the anemone's slimy mucus. The slime works like a camouflage. The anemone won't sting the clownfish because it smells like an anemone!

But other kinds of fish avoid the sea anemone. If they get too close, the sea anemone stings the unwanted visitors with thousands of little darts that line its tentacles. Each one of those harpoons is filled with a paralyzing venom. If a fish tries to catch a clownfish, the clownfish swims into the tentacles. And the hunter scoots off in the other direction!

A clownfish would make an easy meal for a sea anemone. But the anemone won't sting a clownfish. The two animals work together to find food and stay out of danger. Clownfish never swim more than three feet away from their protectors. When a sea anemone kills prey, it shares its meal with its little neighbor. In return for the favor, the clownfish lures in prey, keeps the anemone clean, and bites off diseased tentacles. It bares its teeth and makes loud chattering sounds at butterfly fish that try to eat the anemone.

Two other sea creatures protect themselves with a little help from the anemone. *Hermit crabs* scare off predators by putting anemones on top of their shells. Any animal that tries to eat the crab will be poisoned by the tentacles. *Sea slugs* can eat anemone tentacles without getting sick. They don't destroy the poison darts when they eat them. However, a hungry enemy that eats the slug will get stung by the darts!

## The Cutest Killer

One day, a man was swimming at a beach in Australia. As he waded out of the water, he saw a tiny octopus! Its arms were only 3 inches long. The creature had bright blue rings around its body and was very pretty. The man played with the octopus. He let it slide down his neck and shoulders, then he threw it back into the sea. Two hours later, the man was dead. The *blue-ringed octopus* killed him. The creature had bitten the man's neck and injected him with a tiny, yet deadly, dose of venom.

Because it is so small and beautifully colored, people want to handle the blue-ringed octopus. But this adorable octopus has enough venom in one bite to kill ten grown men.

People think that all octopuses are killers, but the only one that deserves that title is the blue-ringed octopus. Octopuses look frightening— they've got eight incredibly long legs and a huge blob for a head. They have shells inside their bodies. But they won't hurt you. They'd much rather flee than fight if a human swims nearby.

Like anemones, octopuses spend their time feeding on crabs and other small marine creatures. People think that octopuses squeeze their victims to death with their legs, but that's not true. Each leg has 240 suckers that the octopus uses to grab onto food. The suckers stick like glue to the prey.

Just like we use our hands to bring food to our mouths, the octopus uses its arms to bring food to its beak. This beak is shaped like a parrot's. It's strong enough to crush lobster shells. The octopus subdues its victims by injecting poisonous saliva through its beak. However, this saliva isn't strong enough to hurt humans.

## If Looks Could Kill

Many tropical fish found in the Pacific Ocean near Australia are colorful beauties. But not the *stonefish*! It's one ugly creature. Its skin is covered with slime and warts. It's called a stonefish because it looks like a stone. And that's the key to its survival.

This ugly fish lies very still under stones by coral reefs. With its uneven shape and brownish coloring, the foot-long fish looks like a real rock. Even if there's a big fuss going on nearby, the stonefish won't budge. It waits patiently for a meal to swim by. When unsuspecting prey swim close, the stonefish snaps them up in a split second. The movement is so fast, the human eye can't see the catch! Poison is not used to kill the prey.

Stonefish save their venom for defense. Thirteen spiky spines poke out of its back. At the tip of each spine is a sac of venom. Stonefish don't squirt or inject this venom. All they have to do is erect their spines and wait for the enemy—a human or a fish—to step on or rub against their bodies. The spines are sharp enough to cut through flesh and sneaker soles. The slightest amount of pressure squeezes the venom out. The stonefish's sting causes instant, very intense pain, and sometimes even death. Of all the fish in the world, the stonefish is considered to be the most venomous.

## Looks That Fool You

A stingray can grow as big as a bathtub. *Giant stingrays* weigh 750 pounds. That's as much as ten fourth-graders weigh together! The stingray is a close relative of the shark. The stingray is dangerous because of a few stinging spines along its tail, which is longer than its whole body. These spines have several small, very sharp teeth that are covered with venomous slime.

Despite their looks, stingrays aren't aggressive animals. They live quietly on the ocean floor, sucking up worms and shelled animals. They use their powerful stingers only to protect themselves. If danger *is* near, the ray whips its long tail around to sting the enemy. Stingrays sting people for one reason: Swimmers and divers don't see them and step on their tails.

## Eat Me, I Dare You!

If you aren't a speedy swimmer, and you don't have tentacles, stingers, or claws, how do you defend yourself in a sea of hungry predators? If you're a *sea urchin* or *puffer fish*, you turn into a poisonous pincushion.

Sea urchins are round, spiky animals. They aren't fish. Their bodies are covered with spines and tiny jaws that grow on top of stalks. In some species of sea urchins, the spines and jaws are filled with poison. So don't step on those spines!

The sea otter eats the urchin without any problems. It picks up the urchin and cracks its tough shell against some rocks. That way, the otter can eat the urchin's soft insides without getting a mouthful of poison.

If the otter tried that trick with a puffer fish, the otter would die of food poisoning. The puffer fish has poison in its skin and in some internal organs. The poison affects the victim's nervous system, when the victim bites into the puffer fish. In humans, this poison makes people stop breathing. That's why they die.

Unlike the sea urchin, the puffer's spines aren't filled with poison. When the fish is scared, it puffs its body out to make it look very scary. The spines can pierce, but not poison, an enemy's skin.

# 4

## Darts, Warts, and Bites

### This Frog Is No Prince

In the fairy tale, the princess kisses a frog. The frog turns into a prince. The princess was lucky—her frog prince was an everyday pond frog. His back was covered with only slightly poisonous slime that all frogs and toads have. This sort of slime couldn't hurt a human being. If the prince had been a *dart-poison frog,* however, the princess wouldn't have lived to tell the tale.

Dart-poison frogs live in the tropical rain forests of Central and South America. There are about a hundred different species of these frogs. They are amphibians, which means they spend the first part of their lives in water. Like fish, young amphibians breathe through gills and when they become adults they develop lungs. Amphibians have wet skin. The animals stop their skin from drying out on land by secreting slimy sweat. Most frogs have a mild poison in their sweat that affects the muscles and nerves of victims.

Dart-poison frogs do more than keep their bodies moist with their sweat. Their sweat is much more poisonous than any other type of frog sweat and it's useful as a protective device. If a bird or snake pops one of these frogs into its mouth, it will spit the frog right out. Most times, the frog hops away unharmed. If the hunter eats the frog, it will die very quickly. A single dart-poison frog produces almost 2,000 micrograms of poisonous sweat. It takes only 2 micrograms to kill you. (A microgram is one-*millionth* of a gram. A small paper clip weighs about 1 gram.)

The Choco Indians of Colombia have made poison darts from this frog's sweat for hundreds of years. The Indians would tease, even torment, the frogs to make sweat. (Frogs are like humans. They sweat when they're upset.) The sweat isn't clear like ours. It's a white froth. The Indians dip their arrows into the froth. The poison keeps its destructive powers for a year. One frog secretes enough poison to make fifty darts. Whenever the Chocos make poison darts, they protect their hands with leaves so they won't touch the poison. The Chocos use the darts in blowpipes when they hunt birds and mammals. (These days, most Chocos use guns for hunting, but a few still hunt the traditional way.)

Although this poison is very deadly, it's also very helpful. Researchers carefully observe how the poison affects muscles and nerves in lab tests. This helps scientists understand more about how and why our bodies work.

Dart-poison frogs don't look like ordinary green frogs. They come in super-bright colors and patterns. Some are brilliant orange, yellow, or green. Some have stripes or polka dots. They definitely stand out in a crowd, or a rain forest. Its bright colors warn other animals: "Don't eat me, I'm poisonous." The dart-poison frogs are one of the most dramatic examples of warning coloration in the animal kingdom. Most predators will look somewhere else for a meal.

Biologists are very worried that these colorful frogs will become extinct. The frogs are losing their homes because people are destroying rain forests.

## Not-so-tasty Toads

A few years ago, a 5-year-old boy thought it would be fun to pop a toad into his mouth. Ten minutes later, he started drooling and slurring his words. Then his body jerked around in fits. Poison from the *Colorado River toad* caused this. (The boy recovered within a week.)

What's the difference between a frog and a toad? They are actually very similar. In general, a frog has smooth, wet skin and lives near water. A toad has rough skin covered with warts and lives in drier places.

Don't pay any attention to the myth that says you can get warts by touching a toad. But do be careful. The Colorado River toad and the *ma-*

*rine toad* are the two most poisonous toads in North America. They live in the western part of the United States. They don't have poison on their skin, like frogs do. They store it in large lumps above and behind their eyes, and on their thighs. These lumps are poison glands. All true toads store poison this way. When predators or curious people bother the toads, a bad-tasting milky fluid oozes out of these glands. The toxic fluid makes the heart beat faster, irritates the skin, and causes numbness. The poison also stops a person from sweating. Violinists used to rub their hands on toads before concerts. The poison prevented them from getting sweaty palms while playing.

The poison keeps predators like birds and foxes from eating toads. However, many dogs aren't so smart. Each year, about fifty dogs die because they bite into a marine toad. People have died just from eating the marine toad's eggs!

Sugar-cane farmers in the West Indies and Hawaii have used marine toads to keep pesty insects away from their crops. (Toads and frogs eat huge meals of insects.) The toads were so good at their job that farmers in Australia imported them. Unfortunately, toads became pests themselves.

## No Leapin' Lizards

There are over 3,000 species of lizards in the world. Only two are venomous—the *Gila monster* and the *beaded lizard*. These two are good wrestlers but terrible leapers.

These lizards are tough, smart fighters. They move slowly so they don't go after fast-moving prey. That would take too much energy! So they feed on birds, baby animals, and eggs. Clearly, the chances of a person getting bitten by a Gila monster or a beaded lizard are *very* slim!

When these lizards are on the prowl for food, they sniff and taste everything. They're searching for clues to tell them where an animal is hiding.

Once they've tracked down their meal, they don't zap their victims full of venom the way a snake does. These lizards don't have a snake's needle-sharp fangs. Instead, they have venom glands in the lower part of the mouth. The venom flows along a groove to the teeth. When the lizard locks its jaws around the prey, it chews in the venom. The chewing tears up the animal's flesh and makes sure that the venom sinks in. Once, a researcher had to use pliers to make a Gila monster let go of its prey.

Gila monster and beaded lizard venoms affect the nervous system. Usually, venom that affects the nervous system doesn't cause a painful bite. However, a Gila monster bite is very painful.

Are these lizards, toads, and frogs dangerous to humans? Yes and no. Yes, because their venoms and poisons are very strong. No, because all of these creatures find humans pretty boring.

# 5

## Small and Mighty: Deadly Insects

Somewhere in the playground, there's a killer. It doesn't have a knife or a gun. It doesn't have fangs. You'd recognize this killer the minute you saw it. It's small and yellow. It hovers around flowers. It's fuzzy and it buzzes.

The killer is a bee! Every year in the United States, bees and wasps kill twice as many people as snakes kill. Bee venom is weaker than snake venom, yet many people are allergic to bees and wasps. Their bodies swell up like balloons. They can't breathe, so they die.

Of all the insects in the world, only a few are venomous.

### The Jabbers

The *assassin bug* is the size of a freckle. Now

48

how much harm could an insect that tiny do? Amazingly enough, it can easily kill a couple of sheep with its venom. It's one of the world's smallest venomous animals.

Assassin bugs kill prey by jabbing sharp beaks filled with venomous saliva into their victims. The great scientist Charles Darwin probably died from the bite of an assassin bug, but the poison didn't kill him. When they bite, assassin bugs transmit Chagas' disease, which slowly destroys tissue.

Some insects are deadly because of the diseases they transmit, not because of their venomous bite. Mosquitoes have no poison or venom. However, they're probably the deadliest animals in the world. They transmit many fatal diseases such as malaria.

Another good jabber is the *giant water bug*. You know this bug has been around when you find empty frog skins floating on a pond. An excellent swimmer, the giant water bug dives underwater to grab food when it's hungry. It holds its victim with its front legs. When it's got a good grip on its prey, the water bug delivers its deadly bite. The victim is usually a frog or a fish. But sometimes the victim is a big toe! (Don't worry, water bugs can't kill you. They'll just give you a nasty bite.) Water bugs bite for both hunting and defense.

Like the assassin bug, the water bug jabs its huge beak into prey to inject its venom. Water bug venom works like spider venom. It turns the victim's insides into a thick soup. The bug pokes its straw-shaped beak into its prey to suck up supper. Water bugs don't bother to eat the skins of their prey. They leave them behind for scavengers.

Bugs are among the few insects that use venom to catch a meal. All bugs are insects, but not all insects are bugs. A "bug" is a type of insect, just like a cat is a type of mammal.

## Attack of the Killer Bees

Do killer bees really exist? You bet they do! Once a scientist in Costa Rica was snooping around a killer bee hive when a bee stung him. A few seconds later, a cloud of bees chased him as he tried to run away. Hundreds of bees stung him to death. He died in about 15 minutes.

Oh, sure, you think. A cloud of bees? Stories of killer bee attacks sound like something from a horror movie. It's hard to imagine a swarm of bees chasing a person down a road. How could the same animal that makes sweet honey be so fierce?

Killer bees are a species of honeybee. Their real name is *Africanized honeybees*. They live in South and Central America, but they came from Africa. How did an insect from Africa make its way to the other side of the world? In 1957, a scientist in Brazil imported hot-tempered African honeybees so he could breed them with the local, mild-mannered honeybees. The scientist let a queen killer bee out of the lab by accident. Since then, these bees have been slowly moving north at a rate of about 200 miles a year. Killer bees are expected to arrive in the United States sometime in the next few years. Unfortunately, killer bees are upsetting the balance of nature by not pollinating certain plants or by doing it differently from honeybees.

If killer bees sense that you're even *thinking* about getting close to their hive, they'll chase you for over an hour. Like all bees and wasps, killer bees attack victims by injecting venom with needle-sharp stingers. Killer bee venom is actually weaker than other honeybee venom. A single killer bee sting won't kill you. However, 500 stings *will* kill you. And these bees, unlike other bees, frequently attack in huge numbers.

When the first bee stings an invader, it releases a chemical. The instant other bees smell the chemical, they try to sting the invader. All bees and wasps mark invaders with this chemical. Luckily, most of them aren't as quick to attack as the killer bees.

Males don't have stingers; only the females do. Stingers are more than venomous weapons. The female lays her eggs through her stinger. A female honeybee will do anything to protect her hive from honey-licking bears or other intruders. She guards her home with her life. After she stabs her hooked stinger into a victim, she dies. The stinger gets stuck in the animal's skin and is ripped out of her body when she flies away. She dies to keep her hive safe.

This is not true of female *bumblebees* and wasps. They don't die when they sting. Their stinger is shaped differently from that of a honeybee. They can pull it out after a jab. The bumblebee puts on quite a show when she attacks. Not only can she sting many times, she can bite, too! Then she may also roll on her back, stick her stinger in the air, and squirt out venom.

## Invasion of the Fire Ants

Fire ants look like the ants that join you at a picnic, but they sure don't act like them. The fire ant pinches super-strong jaws into its victim's skin and won't let go. When the victim is trapped in its jaws, the ant whips out a stinger at the end of its body. Sometimes the fire ant stings its victims several times. With every sting, the ant injects a very painful venom.

If you get a fire ant bite, your skin feels very itchy at first, then it feels like it's on fire. That's how the insect got its name. One sting is all it takes to kill the centipedes, worms, and dragonflies that fire ants usually hunt. However, fire ants will sting and eat anything on their turf. Like the killer bees, fire ants tend to attack in big groups. When they sting humans, they're stinging in defense. People who are allergic to these bites can get very ill. Once in a while, people die from fire ant stings.

Fire ants are the ultimate pests. They eat anything they can get their little jaws on. They've short-circuited traffic lights by eating away the electrical circuits. They've closed down airports because they've destroyed the runway lights. They've ruined orchards by eating citrus trees. They bite farm workers and kill young calves and other farm animals.

Fire ants first showed up in Mobile, Alabama, about 40 years ago. Now, they've invaded 400 million acres of farmland, parks, playgrounds, and city streets in the United States. And they're taking over more and more land each year. Fire ants aren't great long-distance walkers. They get into the soil of plants that are being transported from one state to another. The ants quickly build mounds in their new home. *Entomologists* (people who study insects) counted 22 million ants in one acre in a field in Florida.

People have tried everything to get rid of these pests. They've tried machines to blow them away. They've tried grinding up their mounds. They've tried over 8,000 different chemicals including poisonous gas to get rid of them for good. Not even electrocution can stop them. Fire ants have invaded the United States, and they're here to stay.

# 6

## Toxic Mammals

Mammals are warm-blooded animals with backbones. They have fur and bear live young. Mammals take care of their babies. The mothers nurse their young with milk. You're a mammal.

Most mammals protect themselves with teeth and claws. Just look at the lion or the wolf.

But some mammals have venom. Two mammals found in Australia, the *platypus* and the *echidna*, have that extra weapon.

The platypus seems like a cross between a duck and a beaver, although it's classified as a mammal. It has fur; it's warm-blooded, and it has a big flat tail like a beaver's. The female nurses her young. Like ducks, the platypus lays eggs, has webbed feet, and spends most of its time in the water. Another strange feature of the platypus is a set of spurs that males have on their back ankles. These half-inch hooks are connected to venom glands in the animal's legs. With a little kick, the platypus can shove the venomous spurs deep into an attacker's flesh. The echidna, or spiny anteater, also has venomous spurs. The echidna and the platypus are the only two egg-laying mammals in the world.

Australia isn't the only place to find venomous mammals. In North America there are *shrews* and *hedgehogs*.

A typical shrew looks like a 7-inch-long fat rat with a pointy snout. It runs around nonstop and always seems to be in a rage. Shrews' red-tipped teeth make them look fierce and bloodthirsty. Like spiders, they paralyze prey much larger than themselves by injecting venom. They deliver their dose of killer saliva with a strong bite.

The shrew will eat whatever is around, including other shrews. Its venom has one ingredient that poisons cold-blooded animals, and another ingredient that poisons warm-blooded animals. If a shrew bites a person, the bite will burn for several hours, but the victim will not die. Shrews live under trash and rotting plants.

Many predators leave the hedgehog alone—its spines scare them off. Badgers and foxes, however, aren't frightened. To keep such predators away, the hedgehog needs poison.

A hedgehog gets its poison from toads. Before munching on a toad, the hedgehog chews the poisonous secretions from the toad's skin. It mixes the poison with saliva, then licks the poison saliva over its spines. The hedgehog is immune to the toad's poison. The hedgehog curls up into a spiky ball when a predator attacks. Or it jumps around and tries to stab the poisonous spines into the attacker. Usually the predator feels too much pain to continue its attack.

# 7

## Uses for Poison

### Poison and Medicine

If you think cough medicine tastes terrible, imagine having to eat *live spiders* when you're sick. That's what people used to do hundreds of years ago in Europe.

Now there's research that shows spiders might save lives. Scientists in Boston, Massachusetts, think that spider venom may prevent brain damage. People with brain disorders from strokes or Alzheimer's disease release a chemical that destroys brain cells. There's a substance in spider venom that stops this chemical from destroying more cells. Scientists are collecting thousands of spiders from Arizona and Utah for more venom tests.

Ancient Egyptians and Chinese used deadly snakes and their venoms to treat diseases. Today, snake venom is still used to cure illnesses. Cobra venom helps relieve severe pain in cancer patients. It's also used to treat arthritis. Venom from the Malayan pit viper dissolves blood clots that cause heart attacks and strokes. Yes, snake venom is a killer. But it may lead us to the cure for many diseases in the future.

What's the best cure for a snakebite? Snake venom. People who've been bitten by a rattlesnake are given a shot of powerful medicine made from rattlesnake venom. This medicine is called *antivenin*. If a cobra bites you, you need medicine made from cobra venom. Snake venoms are different from one another, and therefore need different antivenins.

George Van Horn, a biologist in Florida, helps make antivenin on his farm. This is no ordinary farm. You won't find any cows, sheep, barns, or hay. What you *will* find are fifty different species of venomous snakes from around the world. He raises rattlers, cobras, vipers, and kraits, just to name a few.

Van Horn raises his deadly snakes from the time they're babies. As soon as the babies hatch out of their shells, Van Horn and his workers gently handle the snakes so they can get used to being touched by humans. That way, the snakes won't strike every time a person is near.

Every few weeks, Van Horn and his helpers "milk" the snakes for venom. The snakes must be milked with bare hands! One wrong move could mean possible death. Although the snakes are used to being touched by people, they may still give a horrible bite. Just in case a snake *does* bite during a milking, Van Horn has every snake antivenin in his medicine cabinet.

To collect the venom, Van Horn holds the snake's head over a lab dish to make the snake bite. The dish is covered with a very thin cloth. When it strikes the dish, the snake jams its fangs through the cloth. The cloth soaks up venom that the snake "injects." Afterward, Van Horn removes the venom from the cloth, then freeze-dries it.

To make antivenin, the freeze-dried venom is injected into a horse. (A horse is used because it is a large animal, will produce large amounts of serum, and will remain unaffected by the venom.) The horse's blood produces antibodies to the venom. Antibodies are part of the immune system. They're blood cells that attack and destroy specific foreign cells. Antivenin is horse serum filled with these venom-attacking antibodies.

Antivenins for spider bites, bee stings, and any other type of venomous bites are made the same way.

## Ever Eat a Puffer?

The basic message of this book is clear: Stay away from poisonous creatures and they will leave you alone. However, customs vary from one culture to another. Just because *you* would swim away if you sighted a puffer fish doesn't mean that everyone would. In Japan, people consider raw puffer fish meat to be a delicious treat. People avoid the skin and certain internal organs and eat the flesh where there is a low concentration of poison. A small amount of poison makes a person's lips tingle and makes his or her head feel very light. People take a chance and eat this fish in spite of the deadly risk!

Because of the cobra's great power, many cultures honor and worship this mighty snake. In India, the cobra is called "the ultimate snake." People believe that the powerful spirit Shiva lives inside cobras. A tribe in West Africa also worships the cobra. These people believe that if they honor the snake, it will bless them and grant their wishes. If they anger the snake, it will curse them, make them ill, and cause death.

Other cultures believe that the cobra's potent venom can make a person strong, attractive, and healthy. In Bangkok, Thailand, people eat huge bowls of cobra curry, a spicy stew, to cure all sorts of aches and pains. What would you do if you found cobra curry in *your* lunchbox?!

Poisonous creatures may not be your idea of a scrumptious snack, but they serve an important function in our environment.